I0107474

I AM A BIG GIRL WITH BIG DREAMS!

WHAT MAKES A BIG GIRL?

WILLINA JONES

Copyright © 2025 by Willina Jones.
All rights reserved.
Published by Beyondthebookmedia.com

All rights reserved. No part of this publication may be reproduced, distributed, or transmitted in any form or by any means, including photocopying, recording, or other electronic or mechanical methods, without the prior written permission of the publisher, except in the case of brief quotations embodied in critical reviews and certain other noncommercial uses permitted by copyright law.
For permission requests, write to the publisher, addressed "Attention: Permissions Coordinator," at the address below.

Limit of Liability/Disclaimer of Warranty: While the publisher and author have used their best efforts in preparing this book, they make no representations of warranties with respect to the accuracy or completeness of the contents of this book and specifically disclaim any implied warranties or merchantability or fitness for a particular purpose. No warranty may be created or extended by sales representatives or written sales materials. The advice and strategies contained herein may not be suitable for your situation. You should consult with a professional where appropriate. Neither the publisher nor author shall be liable for damages arising here from.

Beyond The Book Media, LLC
Alpharetta. GA
www.beyondthebookmedia.com

The publisher is not responsible for websites that are not owned by the publisher.

ISNB: 978-1-966430-09-4 (Print)

DEDICATION

To my parents, the late Gerald and Gennie Carmichael, these two parents allowed me to mature into the young lady I am today without judgment and love me unconditionally.

To my friends, who inspired me to go for my dreams, thank you.

To my husband, Bryant Jones, my amazing, gifted children, LaTanya D. Belcher, Earl B. Granger, Evelon M. Granger, and my seven grandchildren, whom I value and love dearly.

To my siblings, who I can't forget, they are my inspiration.

I want to say thank you to my family and friends for believing in me. I couldn't have endured without your love and support.

TABLE OF CONTENTS

OUTLINE

I am an entrepreneur, mother, and wife. I have three adult children and seven grandchildren. As an entrepreneur, I love setting up events, promoting good vibes, and encouraging people. In 2022, God allowed me to restructure my book ministry to another level called Reader Retreat R&R. We sell books and encourage authors to tell their stories and have book signings. I have an online website as well, and we do outreach ministry. My three successful adult children are two daughters and one son aged forty-nine, thirty-nine, and thirty-eight years. My grandchildren, four boys and three girls, are aged 8 to 25. They are my pride and joy. At the age of 54, I remarried after 25 years of being single and waiting for the Lord to bless me. My current husband of 10 years has been my rock in supporting and investing in my ministry and career.

As an entrepreneur, I have dedicated over 20 years to Nina's Christian Book Ministries (NCBM). It began in 2002 at our local Church and within the community, following the Lord's call for me to engage in evangelism. The ministry included a book discussion during Bible class, which inspired and encouraged many participants. Over time, God has transformed the ministry in extraordinary ways, elevating it to new heights. We now host events every three to six months called "Reader's Retreat (R&R)," fostering growth, connection, and inspiration. We do this to build communities and fellowship amongst each other.

As a single woman, it was not easy to navigate this journey. I raised three children and had my first child at fifteen years old. I had to become a responsible adult at a young age. Years later, I had two more beautiful children whom I co-parented. However, I was divorced when my children were four to five years old. I had to become a strong, supportive single mother.

Ministry is my passion; I love to help people and encourage them to be the best version of themselves. At age 48, I focused on my education and returned to school to better myself. It was a challenge because I had grandchildren who were born during that time. However, I made up my mind with God's help to stay persistent on my career goal. I wanted to obtain my associate's degree after trying for many years. There were many distractions, but after 10 years of consistency, I received my associate degree in health information technology in 2024.

Why am I writing this book? I am writing this book to motivate and encourage our generation to have a healthy way of thinking. I have been in the book ministry for many years; I'm passionate about reading and diving into the world of possibility. I struggled with reading and writing in grade school, which always concerned me. Yet, I love reading and writing. It has been difficult for me, and I want to let somebody know we are overcomers. Although reading and writing were my weak points growing up, I am determined to write this book to let someone know they are not alone. Despite difficulties with words, we should never give up on telling our stories.

I am writing this book to inform our generation that anything is possible. Finally, I want young women to believe they can achieve anything they want. Even though life seems to be against us, we are overcomers, and if we keep our faith and depend on God to be our helping hand.

God is my help and my savior that I can depend on. God is the supreme being and the one who created Heaven and Earth. I give him the honor and praise for delivering me as a young lady and maturing my life to be a big girl with his Big dreams.

INTRODUCTION

I was born and raised in Camden, New Jersey, and I have nine siblings. We have a big family, and I have four sisters and five brothers, so you can imagine the size of our family. We had parents who did their best to keep us on track. My mother and father were Christians and believers in Christ Jesus. We grew up in a small neighborhood where families watched out for each other.

Unfortunately, there were times when we got out of control with disobedience to our parents and were in an environment where drugs and drinking were part of our daily lives. I want to talk about myself as a teenager who did not understand life when the enemy tried to destroy me at an early age. At times, I felt discouraged and did not understand myself, and my emotions led me to make a bad decision. I began to develop an addiction to smoking and drinking. Smoking and drinking led me to a hopeless life. Now, boys would try to take advantage of my innocence, and I would avoid them at all costs. However, they got the best of me, and I got pregnant at a young age. My mother told me one day that she apologized that she could not get a chance to inform me about sex. However, it was not her fault; our environment sometimes takes us to places we do not want to go.

Now, at fifteen, I had a baby and was fortunate to have her in my life. Some girls my age had to abort their babies because they were not able to take care of them due to circumstances. My mother was embarrassed because she was a Christian woman, but she embraced the challenge and loved her grandchildren. This situation is crucial because not everyone gets a chance to overcome teenage pregnancy. Being pregnant at fifteen was challenging, and I almost did not return to school after a hot, enjoyable summer.

7

When we returned to school on the second day of class, the principal pulled me over like I was driving one hundred miles an hour. Being pregnant in the seventies was not tolerated in high school; we had to attend a maternity school to take classes. So, it set me back from all the positive activities I was interested in, such as pom-pom girl, majorette like Frances Wyche, marching band like Rosalie Brown, and basketball. As a teenager, your focus should be on loving, playing, and enjoying yourself, but instead, the enemy has a plan for youngsters. However, God is our deliverer, and he has a plan for us. *"For I know the thoughts that I think toward you, saith the Lord, thoughts of peace, and not of evil, to give you an expected end" (Jeremiah 29:11 KJV).* I was back in Church at the age of twenty and serving God. The Bible said, *"Wherefore come out from among them, and be ye separate, saith the Lord and touch not the unclean thing; and I will receive you" (2 Corinthians 6:17 KJV).* My goal was to grow gracefully with God, learn from my immoral behavior, and be an example for my family and friends.

Our society and our families need to focus on helping young ladies value and appreciate themselves and get help understanding who they are. We can capture young ladies and ensure they are thinking positively. Early prevention is key to capturing our young ladies. Our teenagers and adults must know they are loved; we have them at heart. I want young ladies to grow to their full potential and know that resources are available to help them. There are trusted faith-based organizations that can help our youth.

Education and teaching are essential in the lives of our young ladies, but the most important thing is understanding themselves. I noticed in my journey that young ladies lacked their behavior and character. We do not just want to have knowledge and lack credibility in our lives. So, training and teachings are essential in developing excellent characteristics. As a young lady, I had to grow up fast because now I had become a mother and did not know how to act. By the Grace of God, he delivered me. I needed a change because now I have daughters and a son to raise. Life is a series of events that make us grow and appreciate God's grace.

How do you develop your character healthily in today's society? Prayer is essential for all people today. We must build a sense of character to manage it healthily during trials and tests. Our young ladies are falling apart emotionally because they have not been aware of their mental behavior. As young ladies, we must seek help at every age, whether as teenagers or adults. *"But the fruit of the Spirit is love, joy, peace, longsuffering, gentleness, goodness, faith, meekness, temperance: against such there is no law" (Galatians: 5:22-23 KJV).* Character comes from the Greek, which means "I engrave," and is built by the experiences we have as we go through life. Whatever your age or experience, building character is a process of lifelong learning that involves a constant dedication to self-awareness and growth. Be self-aware and understand who you are. (Build Your Character Through Lifelong Learning) It takes time to grow and develop, but I want to motivate and teach our young ladies at a young age. We will experience successes and failures, but we can grow from both. We will encounter many negative and positive situations with different outcomes in life. We must keep our eyes on the prize and never let life get us down. Let us grow up and be the best version of ourselves, regardless of what society tells us we cannot be. I am here to tell you that, yes, you can! Let us refocus and push to be the best we can be.

You should get around a strong community, find what you need for yourself, and ensure your young people get what they need to grow in a healthy environment. Being in the right environment for our young ladies is vital; we must work to make sure our homes are safe. I wanted to ensure my children were in a church community family when they were growing up, as my mother and father did with me. It is challenging for our youth, but we can make it happen. We must stay motivated for the greater good. By the grace of God, I like to promote reading as an outlet from stressful situations. In addition, we have an event every three to six months to read and discuss good books and invite authors to join and share their stories. I desire my business as a book ministry to grow and expand to provide a safe place for young readers to have a positive environment to grow and resources to develop their authentic selves. I consider myself to be that role model as a woman who has and is extending herself to be a big girl now with positive dreams to carry out the call of God on her life. The Bible says, *"Who can find a virtuous woman? for her price is far above rubies" (Proverbs 31:10 KJV)*.

CHAPTER 1

I am a big girl; I like big stuff. This big girl dreams big and does big things. This big girl wants to help motivate young ladies to pursue their dreams and mature to be go-getters, never quit, and be confident as they press and push for their God-given talent. What makes a big girl? Is it her age or weight that makes her big? This big girl is mature and Ambitious, and she never quits. This big girl is a great thinker and strives for excellence. This big girl has been through tough times, and times have made her strong in her pursuits. As a big girl, you must love yourself and believe you are unique. This big girl is confident that God is for her and with her. *"If God is for us, who can be against us?"* The big girl has undeniable dreams and believes in her ability to obtain her goals. Life has been challenging, but do not fear, says the big girl; you can have what you say. *"Now faith is the substance of things hoped for, the evidence of things not seen" (Hebrews 11:1 KJV).* The big girl has imagined authoring her book and reaching for her degree in Health Information Management. The big girl graduated with an Associate Degree in Health Information Technology.

The big girl has experienced a shift in life that compels her to reach for more incredible things. I am excelling and achieving my goals. I am a big girl. The big girl is not perfect, but she strives for perfection because that is what big girls do. Now, accept the challenge, big girl, and go through the process. Someone asked a question about the big girl. Is she big in size? No, she is big in mind, soul, and determination. The big girl is a motivator; she has a big heart and inspires everyone she meets. Her brilliant imagination is bright, and God has inspired her to love books and creative writing. Life is "real" for the big girl, and inspiration is key to success.

The big girl endured challenges as a little girl and had a baby at fifteen. The Big Girl's dreams were shattered, and high school was not a playground for her but a responsibility. The big girl became a mother, and she put on her big pants and did just that. Now, being a mother at a young age was very foggy because the big girl was devastated. Her baby was born prematurely and had to stay hospitalized for a brief time; she did not know what to do. The nurse asked, "Are you coming to see your baby?" She realized a baby was there and present without her mother. The environment the big girl grew up in shaped her in many ways. Her experiences, struggles, and harmful behaviors led her to drink, smoke, take drugs, and engage in sexual activities. However, the big girl received deliverance; God's grace was sufficient, and she accepted Christ at age 20. The big girl could now dream again with God in her life. The big girl was reared in church and eventually returned to Christ.

However, the big girl married at 24 and had two more beautiful children. The big girl has a story. Although her first marriage did not work out, life went on. The big girl is the proud mother of three children, LaTanya, Earl, and Evelon, and seven grandchildren. The big girl is not a quitter but a diligent worker who makes no excuses. The big girl raised her children and perpetually took responsibility for her actions. The big girl did not depend on everyone to take care of her children. The big girl is a go-getter and never quits. The big girl remarried at 54 to a young man named Bryant, a wonderful guy who loves and supports her dreams. God has gifted the big girl tremendously. The big girl has a mission to fulfill. Her determination is relentless, and her book ministry is her passion. God put this book ministry in her heart long ago, and she cannot shake it. Big girl, if you cannot shake it, then shape it.

CHAPTER 2

As a mother, I had to become mature, so I will take the letter M from Mother and use it for a mature one. Yet, as do many others, I became mature at a young age. To display Maturity, one must be willing to accept responsibility for one's actions. "Maturity is the state of maturity." Developing requires time and experience, so do not stop the process. Your life must mature at a healthy pace, so do not be troubled but have a positive drive to go the distance. If you need help, we all must ask, reach out to family, and embrace a circle of strong-minded people. I would not have been an overcomer without the circle of family and friends. My family and church played an intrinsic part in my growth as we participated in church activity groups, such as choir, traveling to various churches, and youth events. We must surround our young adults in a positive environment so they can be healthy as they mature into adulthood. As mothers, let us allow Maturity to grow, accept responsibility, and embrace our God-given ability and talent to be mature go-getters.

THREE TRAITS OF MATURITY

1. Self-awareness: "Maturity grows from a seed of awareness; an awareness of the self and the actions you take. Being self-aware means you are able to look at yourself through the eyes of an observer. You can take a somewhat neutral stance to watch your thoughts, actions, and emotions before applying a rational filter to them. Essentially, self-awareness is about building up an understanding of your personality; its strengths and weaknesses, its potential and limitations, and every little nuance" (Phillips-Waller, 2023).

2. Humility: "Even though you appreciate the importance of each decision you take, you remain a humble and modest person. You never take yourself to be above others, regardless of your status, wealth, power, or influence. You know that, when it comes down to it, we are all born equal and we all die equal. You refrain from letting any personal success go to your head and you treat people fairly and respectfully whatever capacity it may be" (Phillips-Waller, 2023).

3. Accountability: "When you reach a certain level of Maturity, you grasp what a great responsibility it is to be human. You accept that we are all accountable for our own choices and the wider impact they may have on the world. The belief that things happen to you is eroded and replaced with a proactive mindset that understands the consequences of your actions. No longer will you live passively among the world; you take strides to change your situation where necessary so that you can live conscientiously." (Phillips-Waller, 2023).

CHAPTER 3

Do you consider yourself a go-getter? I am a big girl with a big dream, so I work hard to succeed in doing my best. Go-getters are doers who work to develop themselves in any way possible. "Go-getters are defined as an aggressively enterprising person." I did not always know that it would take hard work with no excuses. I was working to survive day in and day out. Sometimes, I had to work two jobs to make ends meet for my family and did not complain. I desired to get an education to better myself; through education, I want to impact others so they can do it, too.

My favorite scripture is *"I can do all things through Christ which strengtheneth me" Philippians 4:13 KJV)*. Working hard produces a work ethic. As an ambitious person, you must keep up with the pace of life and not give up so quickly. My work ethic has been a journey, and sometimes you wonder why you must work so hard, and others get it easily. God blessed me to work and find good jobs. Although they were temporary, the Lord favored me through my employers. Also, I like helping people find work and have recommended jobs to others. God's gift is to encourage and promote others by faith that a job or career is there for them.

One day, I became aware of my situation. I was working hard and not accomplishing anything. I am not the smartest, but I needed more than making ends meet. Also, I realized that no one would do this for me but me. For years, I put everything and everybody first, working two jobs and running back and forth on errands for everybody. My education was at risk, and I said that because I could not even write a complete sentence or could hardly spell. I found myself working hard for the boss and was not appreciated. My boss gave me good criticism one day, and I took it positively and thanked her. At that time, I was working two jobs and told myself, "This is it. I am going back to school." So, guess what? I went part-time to that job, applied to college at 48, and started basic skills from the bottom up. It was a challenge. The writing was so interesting to me when I started college right after high school, but I could not get it. So, I went back and took English Composition I.

The professor passed the grades around the class, and mine said I must retake. So, I went to the school, paid for the retake, and told the guidance counselor. While she looked up my grades, I told myself I couldn't do this anymore. However, the counselor came back confused about why I'd paid to retake the class; I'd received an A in the class.

From that day to this, I knew I could do it. So, I kept going until I finished. After ten years, God did it, and I am so proud of myself. I am on a mission to write my first book and believe in God. To the reader, do not give up. You are a go-getter. Now, let God develop you into the person he intends for you to be. Do not quit because quitting is not an option. *"Know ye not that they which run in a race run all, but one receiveth the prize? So run, that ye may obtain" (1 Corinthians 9:24 KJV).*

CHAPTER 4

Push and press for power; this method will bring about change. God wants the best for our lives. So, let us push for our purpose, press for our prosperity, and walk in power. To push and press for power is called perseverance. "Perseverance is defined as persistence in doing something despite difficulty or delay in achieving success." Health is wealth, and we must push to obtain and support our purpose of healthy living.

You may ask yourself many questions, and the answers are inside of you, but it takes perseverance and believing in yourself. Let us be persistent because we know nothing comes easy. Do not worry about the time it will take care of itself. The Bible said, *"Take therefore no thought for the morrow for the morrow shall take thought for the thing of itself sufficient unto the day is the evil thereof" (Matthew 6:34 KJV).*

We must push and pursue our God-given talent and not fear what is for us. I would be satisfied to encourage someone as I live this life. Some of you may ask, "How?" The answer is to keep moving and believing that God is in control. Preparation is another powerful P word. Prepare for your now. Preparing can be difficult, but bringing order to your life is necessary. God gave me a vision in 2020, and I did not understand it because I thought it was a message to preach. But he said the power of the P's push, press for power. I shared the power of the Ps with my grandson, and I hope they will remember to push for power and be positive.

I have been pushing these last days, and power has confronted me. I am excited for the push and the press that answered my heart's desire. Remember the olive tree; you must go through the press to get oil. Pressing is not an easy task because of our imperfections or wrinkles. Keep pressing. The oil is about to be released. Pressing takes time, so prepare for the journey. If it is easy, it has not gone through the test or the press. I must go through the tests to be all that I can be. Pressing is a must because it makes oil, and oil is priceless. "In the Bible, the olive tree is a powerful symbol of God's blessings, provision, and protection. It is often used to represent peace, prosperity, and the presence of the Holy Spirit. The olive tree is mentioned numerous times in both the Old and New Testaments and is often associated with the land of Israel and the Jewish people" (The Olive Tree, 2024). Pushing and pressing for power is a method of success. Keep pressing; it is worth it—the power of the P's: Push, Press, and Power.

CHAPTER 5

Have you ever heard a person say I do not have confidence? Confidence is vital to have so you can achieve your goal. You will always be evaluated in your confidence because of rejection, but do not worry; you can succeed if you believe in yourself. Believing in yourself will take you far and help you overcome many situations. If I had not been confident, I would not have graduated from college after 10 years. Regardless of how long it took, I had to believe in myself; we could have wished it had happened sooner. God knows best. Remember, your life is in his hands; He knows what is best for us. Trust in yourself to be your best.

As strong women, we must keep pushing and believing that we can succeed, no matter the task. So, let's build that confidence like a builder putting up a building with structure and the right tools to do so. We do not have confidence because we lack the tools to grow our mindset. We will obtain those tools to start building our lives as we intend, one stone at a time. Make sure the stone is the right size for the right moment; every decision is essential. Every stone in your life is precious, so let's refine those areas to build confidence to be impacted by society and make a change for continued growth. Take time to reflect on what confidence is genuinely about because we will need it in life to go to the next level. Let's stop and meditate on the scripture, Philippians 3:13: "Brethren, I count not myself to have apprehended: but this one thing I do, forgetting those things which are behind, and reaching forth unto those things which are before." (KJV).

Here are five ways to challenge your confidence:
1. Celebrate your successes.
2. Take a class.
3. Say positive things.
4. Celebrate other people.
5. Encourage yourself.

We must exercise confidence to grow, mature, be that big girl, and have big dreams. I am that confident woman. I am a big girl with big dreams because things are possible. Everything is not working out as I wanted it to. But everything is working for my good. Trails come to make us strong, and I am getting stronger every day.

"When you feel confident, you are more likely to succeed because confidence activates brain circuits that produce an elevated mood, lower anxiety, and sharper thinking — all of which raise the odds of success, Robertson said. These are the same brain circuits that get activated when you do succeed. So, whether you have confidence or succeed, even at a small task, it leads to success and then even more confidence" (Robertson).

CHAPTER 6

For me, quitting is not an option. I refuse to entertain the thought because a love for victory drives me. No matter the challenges, I choose to persevere. So, I encourage you: don't give up and never quit. There is always another level waiting for you to reach—despite the odds, you can rise higher and achieve greatness.

In a world filled with negativity, it's time to fight back—not just against the negative vibes but also against the adversary, who seeks to discourage and defeat God's children. The Bible reminds us: *"Be sober, be vigilant; because your adversary the devil, as a roaring lion, walketh about, seeking whom he may devour" (1 Peter 5:8 KJV).*

We are winners by design, created to overcome and thrive. So, my declaration for you today is this: you are a winner. Believe it, embrace it, and never quit.

Today, you are the winner!

Everybody is winning around me.

Today, I won.

Today is my day.

I am on the winning side.

Today is my day to believe.

Today is the day I recognize my value.

It is my day to contribute to society.

Today is my day to conquer all.

Today, you are the winner!

I have what it takes.

God made me, too!

I am going all in because today is the day

I am changing my mindset.

I am an overcomer.

Today is a new outlook for me.

Today, I am wearing my new lenses.

I am changing my stand.

I am a winner, oh yes.

Today I am free.

Today, I am rich.

Today, I am going to write my book.

Today, God is going to open doors.

Today, I am going to receive my promise.

Today is the day.

I am leaving all my problems behind me.

I am going full force.

I am reaching a mentality toward a winner.

I am dancing, but you do not see my feet moving.

I am shouting, but you do not see me hollering.

I am pressing toward a winner's trophy.

My eyes are on the prize.

Today I won.

*"I can do all things [which He has called me to do] through
Him who strengthens and empowers me [to fulfill
His purpose—I am self-sufficient in Christ's sufficiency; I am
ready for anything and equal to anything through Him who
infuses me with inner strength and confident peace."
- Philippians 4:13 ABV*

CHAPTER 7

I am a big girl with a big dream. If you can't dream, then what? Dreams and imagination are good things for the human mind. I am the type of person who loves to dream and imagine the impossible. I am optimistic and like to look on the bright side of the equation. Growing up as a youth was interesting because I was around older folks, and it seemed like I could not do what I desired. Don't get it twisted. I respected my elders and their words of wisdom, but I knew it was something that I could do with their guidance. I remember my oldest sister saying, "You aren't grown," and she would say it yearly on my birthday. Also, I was used to hearing, "You are not grown" until one day, at about 40 years old, on my birthday. I asked my sister if I was grown yet, and she said, "You have grown."

I always felt I had to prove something to everybody. In other words, I was a misfit and sometimes misunderstood. God called me to ministry, and my former pastor, Pastor Thompson, said, "You're an evangelist." I know I have a special gift from God. I like motivation and motivational speakers. In our society today, we need more motivation. The Bible, to me, is here to motivate us and keep us encouraged because this life is challenging.

I remember my late brother, Gerald, who encouraged me during the six months of his life when he lived with me. He told me what I was capable of, encouraged me, and made me aware that I am a big girl and greatness is within me. I said, "Please, Gerald, I can't do that." I was out of a job and didn't know what I was going to do. My brother said, "I know someone at Hahnemann Hospital who can help." He asked me to give him my resume, and even though I was surprised, my spirit led me to give it to him. He encouraged me, and I did find a good job making $5,000 more than any of my previous positions.

It was another time when we were discussing a problem in the house, and he said, "You know what you are doing. You raised your children; you have your home. I trust your judgment." I felt so empowered by that statement. We must be careful not to let the enemy keep us bound.

We can't be intimidated by our surroundings when we know it's our time to grow. When you are growing to another level, you must stay focused. You are leaving the past behind because you see a greater future for yourself. I will never forget one day I was walking, and I saw a sign that read no detour, and the spirit asked me, "What would you do if there were no detour?" I said I would go around or go up. I was not going back. I jotted these words down while trying to understand the detour sign.

One day, a release came, and I made that detour. The journey was fulfilling, and I made the best of what I thought was right. I gave people the benefit of the doubt. I was just a young girl, and I followed my dreams. I loved the Lord because he first loved me. I trusted God, followed His people, and stayed connected, but one day, God released me. I did not release myself. I was beginning to feel like the road was ending. I had to be encouraged to do this at this time in my life.

I believe in God for my journey. Sometimes, you must turn the page when that chapter is closed. Be encouraged on your next journey to greatness. I will never forget when I came across a book called Think and Grow Rich: A Black Choice by Dennis Kimbro and Napoleon Hill. This book changed my way of thinking to another level. Those great pioneers inspire me in this book, and I believe that success is possible. Listen to this: "Very few people have learned to use imagination to its fullest potential. Society teaches us that it is not adult to fantasize. Too many of us have learned society's lesson so well that we never daydream; our imaginations rust away from lack of exercise" (Hill, 1991).

Keep dreaming, big girl, and be encouraged. The Bible says David encouraged himself. *"And David was greatly distressed; for the people spake of stoning him because the soul of all the people was grieved every man for his sons and for his daughters; but David encouraged himself in the Lord his God"* (1 Samuel 30:6 KJV).

It's okay to be motivated. You have a great talent within you, so dig deep inside of yourself and move to your full potential. I am challenging myself as much as I can. I am encouraged to build myself from here to there and expect a change in my future. Whether it is spiritual, career, or family, I am going the distance. We must first believe in ourselves. Most people don't think they can have what they say. "Your life-changing choice may be to switch careers, to leave an abusive relationship, to go back to school, to stop drinking, to adopt a child, to start a business, to lose weight, to start a charity… to name a few. If you dare to do so, you could make any one of those choices today. And you would change your life" (Anderson, 2008). If I can encourage you to stay motivated, I have evangelized the world in just a few words. Keep going and never quit; you've got this. The big girl believes in you, so take your position for greatness.

CHAPTER 8

What does earning first place mean? When I think of *first place,* I think of a challenge to someone who was maybe in a competition. I think of the athletes who compete on a team or play a game to accomplish a win. There is nothing wrong with competing if it is fair and you work hard for it. I am a big girl and a hard worker, believing in earning my position. I remember my friend who told me to hold my head up when I received my degree because I earned it. Also, he told me not to feel intimidated because I put the work in. I said to myself years ago that I wanted to do my best, study hard, and do my assignments.

The Bible talks about running the race. *"Know ye not that they which run in a race run all, but one receiveth the prize? So run, that ye may obtain. And every man that striveth for the mastery is temperate in all things" (1 Corinthians 9:24-25 KJV).* Earning takes focus and being temperate in your pursuit of excellence, because first-place winners are persistent and don't give up easily. Whether you are in first, second, or third place, keep going because winning takes time.

Hold your position, stay humble, and know that what you have earned is valuable. Nobody gave you anything; you earned it through your obedience, endurance, and perseverance. Fight for your beliefs, and don't accept what the enemy is trying to sell you. You are bigger and better than what you give yourself credit for. Ask me how I know; people see more in you than you see in yourself.

Trust and believe that you are the one for the position. You are the one for the part. God has made room for all of us. Now, let's make room in our hearts for Him. You are the first-place winner in God's eyes. Through dedication, you have earned your place in society for all the effort you have made to create a safe place in your life. The rewards you have earned and are earning are yours, so be proud of yourself.

CHAPTER 9

Building character means everything as a big girl with dreams. Imagine a lady who has everything going for herself -- family, husband, children, and career. She had an inheritance, but she had to portray good character and work hard. Character is not a given, but you must work on yourself.

Have you ever heard the saying, "Good things come to those who wait"? Patience is a good characteristic to have. In society today, we do not see patience as being too familiar. Character is key to a successful life because you can go around and exist, but you should be thriving, and for that to happen, you must believe in yourself. A girl with dreams should build her character and portray good qualities.

Big girls are mature because they have been through some struggles in life and have chosen to perfect themselves by declaring I am a big girl with big dreams. Here are some good characteristics in the Bible: love, joy, peace, kindness, self-control, and faithfulness. It's essential to carry these characteristics in your life.

Work on yourself to better your life despite your enemy. The enemy fights us daily, but we must fight back because our future is vital to the next generation. Life is not just about you but about everything you consist of. Your value is essential to being that big girl with big dreams. Keep your faith so you can succeed and live to your full potential.

I pray that you become all God intended for you to become and that all our dreams will become a reality. Search inside yourselves, find your truth, and work hard. Most of all, our lives will be pleasing to God, and He can make us big girls with big dreams.

Here are The 7 Steps to Building Character:

1. Self-reflection: "The first step towards building character is to engage in regular self-reflection. By examining your thoughts, feelings, and actions, you gain a deeper understanding of your values, strengths, and weaknesses. This insight allows you to identify areas for growth and set goals that align with your true intentions and resolve." (Ocean, 2024)

2. Develop self-discipline: "Character growth requires self-discipline, which involves consistently choosing to do what is right and necessary even when it is difficult. By cultivating self-discipline, you develop the ability to control your impulses and emotions, enabling you to make choices that align with your values and goals." (Ocean, 2024)

3. Embrace challenges: "Challenges provide opportunities for growth and self-discovery, pushing you to test your limits and develop resilience. By embracing challenges, you learn how to face adversity, adapt to change, and develop problem-solving skills, all of which contribute to building character." (Ocean, 2024)

4. Practice authentic communication: "Expressing your thoughts and feelings honestly and openly is crucial to building character. Authentic communication allows you to align your speech with your intentions, fostering trust and respect in your relationships. By being true to yourself and others, you demonstrate integrity and build a strong foundation for character growth." (Ocean, 2024)

5. **Cultivate a positive attitude:** "Your attitude shapes how you perceive and respond to challenges and setbacks. Cultivating a positive attitude enables you to approach difficulties with optimism and resilience, making it easier to overcome obstacles and grow from your experiences. A positive attitude also influences your personality, making you more approachable and likable to others." (Ocean, 2024)

6. **Nurture relationships:** "Building character involves nurturing relationships with others, as they provide support, guidance, and opportunities for growth. By cultivating strong connections with friends, family, and community members, you develop empathy, compassion, and a sense of responsibility to others, which contribute to your overall character development." (Ocean, 2024)

7. **Maintain accountability:** "The final step in building character is maintaining accountability for your actions and decisions. By holding yourself accountable, you demonstrate integrity and ensure that your thoughts, speech, and actions align with your values and goals. This process helps you grow from your mistakes, learn from your experiences, and continue on your journey towards ABV. (n.d.). Amplify Bible Version.

I AM A BIG GIRL WITH BIG DREAMS!

WHAT MAKES A BIG GIRL?

www.ingramcontent.com/pod-product-compliance
Lightning Source LLC
Chambersburg PA
CBHW051741040426
42447CB00008B/1245